CW01418370

Lifeboat #15

Lifeboat #15

L. E. Johnson

authorHOUSE®

AuthorHouse™
1663 Liberty Drive
Bloomington, IN 47403
www.authorhouse.com
Phone: 1-800-839-8640

© 2012 by L. E. Johnson. All rights reserved.

No part of this book may be reproduced, stored in a retrieval system, or transmitted by any means without the written permission of the author.

Published by AuthorHouse   10/25/2012

ISBN: 978-1-4772-6967-1 (sc)
ISBN: 978-1-4772-6969-5 (hc)
ISBN: 978-1-4772-6968-8 (e)

Any people depicted in stock imagery provided by Thinkstock are models, and such images are being used for illustrative purposes only.

Certain stock imagery © Thinkstock.

This book is printed on acid-free paper.

Because of the dynamic nature of the Internet, any web addresses or links contained in this book may have changed since publication and may no longer be valid. The views expressed in this work are solely those of the author and do not necessarily reflect the views of the publisher, and the publisher hereby disclaims any responsibility for them.

Table of Contents

Lifeboat # 15

For 100 years, one lingering mystery

surrounding *Titanic* remained unsolved

. . . until <u>NOW</u>.

NEVER BEFORE TOLD STORY in its entirety

The true story of the man from steerage who was shot at six times as he
attempted to jump into Lifeboat #15 while ship personnel were shouting,

"Women and Children Only!"

He lived to tell this story . . . others were shot and thrown overboard.

Bert Johns . . . during his time in
Marlette.

"THE TITANIC"

A children's campfire song

First verse and chorus

Oh, they built the ship TITANIC to sail the ocean blue,

And they built it so the water wouldn't come through,

But the good Lord raised his hand,

Said, "This ship will never land".

It was sad when the great ship went down.

Oh, it was sad . . . too bad.

It was sad when the great ship went down

To the bottom of the sea.

Husbands and wives, little children lost their lives.

It was sad when the great ship went down.

DEDICATION:

To two old gentlemen who taught me to enjoy a good story:

Earl Ingram and Ward Atkins

And to one old gentleman whose life **_WAS_** the story:

Bert Johns

THANKS TO:

Library of Congress—for their invaluable assistance supplying dozens of 100-year-old *Titanic* interviews taken as survivors departed the *Carpathia*. These were mainly from smaller local papers not generally read in 100 years.

Marlette Township Library

Glen & Carol Jamison

Jean Morgan

Jean Kempa

The Port Huron Area family of Bert Johns

Special thanks:

Dennis & Sue Shoemaker

Cover design:

Lois Johnson & Sue Shoemaker

Around the time of 1987 when we started the Marlette Historical Society, Marlette attorney Ward Atkins and Marlette businessman Earl Ingram confided in me the story of a local Marlette man who had sailed on the Mighty *Titanic's* maiden voyage. Although they knew him well as a successful local businessman, little was known about this man other than the fact that he had been on *Titanic*. Of the dozens of steerage passengers who attempted to survive that night, apparently he was the only man who was shot but lived. He was very ashamed but wanted the true story told, the only stipulation being that it not be published until 50 years after his death. This was done in the local history book of Marlette, IMAGES-MILLENNIUM EDITION. I have never seen his story in any books about *Titanic*. So, this is Bert Johns' story.

His name was Bert Johns. You won't find that name on the passenger manifest anywhere. He changed his name immediately upon arriving in America to stop the harassment. According to every book I've ever read or seen on the Sinking of *Titanic*, everyone talked about him but no one knew him . . . no one saw him . . . everyone saw him . . . he was the man whom no one could say for sure that they actually saw . . . the man who was shot but must have died like all the other men from steerage when they tried to get into a lifeboat . . . the man who dared to jump into a lifeboat filled with women and children while the ship's officers were crying out "Women and Children Only" . . . the one shot six times but no one could confirm this. Every person on *Titanic* told a different story of that night, and of shots heard, and of men trying to get into the lifeboats.

I always assumed that everyone knew of Bert Johns, the man who was shot jumping into that lifeboat and covered with the women's skirts and lived to tell about it. But nowhere was his name ever mentioned . . . until the advent of the Internet.

The answer to this puzzle is very interesting.

What's in a name?

Bert Johns

Borak Hana Assi

Hamah or Hanne

Mubarik Hanna Sulayman AbicAsa

Barak Hannah

Hanna Moubarak

Hanna Monbarek

Hanna Assi Barah

John Borak

John Barak

Moubarch

Maubarek

Borek

Johns

Hardine

Barack Hussein

John Boak Hanna Monbarek

~All names given for Bert Johns in *Titanic* books or articles ~

BIOGRAPHY OF BERT JOHNS

Born in Hardin, Lebanon (Syria) on April 10, 1885, Bert Johns boarded *Titanic* on its 90-minute stop at Cherbourg, France, on April 10 at 9:00 p.m. as a 3ʳᵈ class passenger, with his destination Wilkes-Barre, Pennsylvania. He escaped the sinking on Lifeboat #15 which they were sending off with empty seats. He was shot and left for dead, hidden beneath the skirts of the ladies in his boat. He married Miss Elizabeth Hassey on July 16, 1912. He was one of the few 3ʳᵈ Class men who survived the crash and sinking of the Queen of the Seas, the $10,000,000 ship considered "Unsinkable" . . . the Mighty *Titanic*. The grandest ship ever made was 883 feet long, furnished to the nines on every level . . . Turkish baths, palm gardens, gymnasiums, each level somewhat classier than the Class the ticket owned, leaving each and every passenger in total and absolute awe at the luxury throughout the entire ship. Some Second Class people declared that the accommodations in Second Class on *Titanic* were equal to First Class on any other ship.

Bert Johns remained unmoving on the floor of the lifeboat until they were rescued by the *Carpathia* and ultimately landed in New York. He went to his brother's in Port Huron, Michigan, working in industrial plants for the next three years. Eventually he moved to the small town of Marlette, in the Heart of the Thumb of Michigan, where he opened up a cigar and candy store on Main Street, just four doors down from the Opera House. Marlette was about as far removed from the sinking of *Titanic* as he could get. He returned after 15 years in Marlette to Port Huron where his brother's family lived, and opened a fruit store on Quay Street. He eventually quit that business and went into the tavern business with Bert's Tavern located on 622 Water Street. He was a member of St. Steven Catholic Church and died on February 2, 1952, at his home at 216 Broad Street after a short illness of one month.

Bert Johns was survived by two sisters, Mrs. Peter Simon and Mrs. Peter George, both of Kingston, Pennsylvania, and two brothers, Simon and Alex Johns.

The iceberg suspected of sinking *RMS Titanic*; a smudge of red paint much like *Titanic's* stripe was seen near the base. (Wikipedia)

ICEBERG

Long, long ago, before humans first walked the earth, thousands and thousands of ages past, Greenland had been slowly changing from just soil to snow-covered mountains. The mammoth and silent *Titanic* iceberg, formed eons ago, had been on its journey from the mountains of Greenland to meet its destiny with DEATH on that cold April night of 1912 . . . its FATE sealed just like the huge ship it had been awaiting to meet to send to the bottom of the sea, like a used and broken toy, to be forgotten after time by many, as it lay in its sea coffin.

As the soft, virgin white snow began falling onto the lands of Greenland, the mountains were soon covered with layers and layers of it. Century upon century the mountains accepted the fluffy white snow until the mammoth weight of it caused the snow on the bottom to become ice. These rivers of ice became what we call glaciers today. Eventually these rivers started moving down the mountain, into the valleys and on their way to the seas. The force of the immense weight they carried kept this mass moving on and on, so powerful that nothing could stay in its way. The glaciers actually moved only a few feet each year, but in time reached the sea and into the water. As it was partly into the water, the coastline gave way and broke off, with its massive piece becoming an iceberg.

When a glacier breaks it is said that it makes a noise louder than anything on earth. The broken off pieces become icebergs. Some of these chunks of iceberg then float southward until the warm water causes them to melt. Our iceberg was part of a glacier of mammoth size. Once it hit the water and separated from the glacier, this prehistoric iceberg now began to speed up on its journey to a date with DEATH on that April night in 1912, a journey of millenniums of time. Circumstances would pull together and place the mighty ocean ship on a collision course with its Destiny. The iceberg and the innocent Ship of Dreams collided and the great ship only needed one hit to make it crumple and fall two miles to its current resting place at the bottom of the sea.

Dividing into many icebergs yearly, the famous Humboldt glacier would give birth to enough bergs to match the State of New Jersey in size. The North Atlantic icebergs wreak havoc on sailors between Cape Farewell and Cape Race, where the icebergs from the east and west coasts of Greenland come together. In modern times, these bergs move very slowly and silently, stalking like a pack of jackals ready to pounce, as they lay in wait for a tasty ocean liner.

The actual size of an iceberg is difficult to discern, as most of it is underwater. The closer and closer one gets to the iceberg, it begins to look smaller and smaller. However, estimates say that the iceberg itself widens out just under the surface for thousands of feet each way, waiting patiently for any ship to meet it on a foggy night.

A range of 50 feet to 300 feet seems to be average, although some of these sea monsters can actually be several miles in length. The largest iceberg ever seen was over nine miles long. It stretched side to side over 1000 yards, and was 200 feet high. It was said that April night in 1912 the infamous iceberg that hit *Titanic* was over 80 feet high, as reported by Robert W. Daniels of Philadelphia to questioning in the government query, as he told of a terrific crash, the lights going out, the boat quivering.

E. Z. Taylor of Philadelphia awoke by a dull and grinding crash, which was not enough to frighten him. He continued to describe the hit this way, "I saw the iceberg we struck, and it was fully 80 feet high above the water. It seemed to me that when we struck it we passed over part and under part, as if below the floor and ceiling of a room. The sea was as smooth as glass."

A White Star Company official told in the Newark papers the scene as it was that night. "From reports that have come in it is evident that *Titanic* went down after a death grapple with the hidden 'spines' of the iceberg. These spines, sharp and jagged, ripped her bottom just like the tender side of a greyhound might be snagged by a steel spur." He continued by saying that the design of *Titanic* was so built that she could be turned into 30 watertight steel boxes within thirty seconds. "There is no doubt that in this instance the bulkheads of *Titanic* were locked within a few seconds of the first crash. I say first crash because I believe there were a series of impacts. I believe the ship fought the berg until she went down." . . . "The *Titanic*, speeding along at seventeen or eighteen knots, was impaled upon this jagged projection, which held her. At the same time the iceberg approached rapidly and rammed her. After the first impact, I believe the *Titanic* was forced back, but that this, combined with the force of her reversed engines, was sufficient to release her from the clutch of the under-water 'spines'. These spines probably held the gigantic craft until the ever-advancing mass of ice struck her again. All the while the spines were ripping apart the **Titanic's** bottom. Finally they rowelled the entire length of the vessel. At the same time the walls of the side bulkheads were probably being battered in by huge chunks of ice which were constantly falling."

The official of the White Star lines continued in the interview on April 18, 1912, with the Newark Times, "The underwater projections at last succeeded in ripping huge holes in the bottom of the vessel. The water rushed in, putting out the fires and flooding the engine and power rooms. This probably cut off power for the wireless apparatus and also plunged the huge craft into pitch darkness."

THREE SISTERS

The Gems of the Ocean
Three Sister Ships, Three Mysterious Tragedies

In the first decade of the 20th Century the massive super ocean liners ruled the world. The passenger ships were owned and run by the White Star Line, while the Cunard Line carried freight.

The White Star Line had originally foreseen a set of three spectacular ocean liners flying their flags across the North Atlantic Ocean carrying three types of passengers. They were to be the *Olympic*, *Titanic* and the *Gigantic*.

White Star's intent was to grab the regular TransAtlantic westbound tide of immigrants coming to America. It was an unceasing flow of people bound for a new life in the United States. The First Class travelers gave the ship invaluable publicity. People love the Society pages. Everyone was in awe at the boxes and boxes and suitcase after suitcase, and the clothes and the jewels and furs of the grand ladies and their gentlemen, so crowds gathered from all over for the launching.

Titanic was the largest and grandest ship ever. She held many secrets . . . she was the most luxurious. She only had one ride in her . . . but what a ride it was!

Olympic was the first and the world's largest ship (until *Titanic*). Later during the war a submarine rammed her and sank her.

Gigantic had not yet been built when the Queen of the Seas went down. White Star Lines officials decided that "*Gigantic*" sounded too arrogant. They were already being accused of overdoing and bragging about it. *Gigantic* was renamed after the sudden demise of *Titanic*. She

5

was called the *Brittanic*. Were the Three Sisters doomed? The *Brittanic* was sunk in the war in the Mediterranean by a sudden massive explosion. She sank in 1 hour, ambushed by a German torpedo.

There was always a big competition between Cunard and White Star. The Cunard Line's ships included the *Luisitania* and *Moritania*. They went for speed. The *Luisitania* could make a 3,300 mile trip in 4 days 19 hours. White Star was size and luxury—a passenger ship while Cunard shipped freight.

Cunard was ruled by speed, while White Star allowed luxury and greed over common sense.

PREVIOUS BIG SEA DISASTERS

Newark News

Disasters That Have Befallen Great Ships in Recent Years

The wreck and sinking of the world's greatest ocean liner ever on its maiden voyage sent shock waves throughout the world. The terrifying disaster overwhelmed the seafaring community as well as the rest of us. Confidence was at an all-time low, although *Titanic* was certainly <u>not</u> the exception to the rule . . . just perhaps the most famous.

The Anchor liner *Columbia* smashed into an iceberg on August 2, 1911. Once again the iceberg won. The dusk collision off Cape Race left the ship badly injured. Literally tons of ice fell onto the ship, but no one was fatally injured.

The *Kronprinz Wilhelm* met its fate in 1908, another dusk mishap. She was at reduced speed at the time of the collision, so she was able to slink into port two days later.

A great loss of lives occurred in April of 1873. The steamship *Atlantic* foundered in a storm off Halifax with 600 aboard, with 546 missing.

Pomerania sank in the English Channel after a collision November 26, 1878. Dead: 46.

The Cunard's *Oregon* sank 18 miles east of Long Island. Interestingly enough, she collided with another steamer. It was a hit and run—no one ever accepted responsibility, and no lives were lost, as the ship remained floating for eight hours.

The steamer *Elbe* collided with another steamship *Cathrie,* and the North German liner went down with 330 on board. (January 20, 1895)

In March of 1897, the French ocean steamer *Ville de St. Nazaire* caught fire and burned to the water's edge. It was during a violent storm. No one could reach the ship, so forty people lost their lives.

The *Aden* went down with a loss of 78 people off the east coast of Africa in June of 1907.

Cromartyshire rammed the steamer *La Bourgoyne* causing it to sink near Sable Island on July 4, 1898, losing all the crew and passengers numbering 535.

Seven hundred fifty souls died when the steamship *Norge* sprung a leak.

Off the coast of Holland the steamer *Berlin* was wrecked with a loss of one hundred fifty on February 21 of 1907.

Three hundred Chinese were drowned when a Chinese steamer foundered off the harbor of Hong Kong on July 28, 1808.

Two ocean liners went down, no collision, leaving a double tragedy with hundreds of lives lost, off the coast of South America. They were the *Prudentia* and the *Folgefounden.*

San Pablo sank off the Philippines on November 27, 1908, with 100 dead.

Modern technology has aided in saving lives in the 20th Century . . . the wireless could have and should have saved the mighty **Titanic**. Human error can never be completely overcome. The *Florida* collided with the steamer *Republic* on January 24, 1909. Ships responding to the wireless call got all but eight people off before it sank.

INSURANCE

London, England April 15

Although the Ship of Dreams cost and was basically valued at $10,000,000, it was insured for only $5,000,000. Of that amount the White Star ran the risk of the first $750,000 of damages, with the underwriters only meeting any claim in excess of that amount. The cargo alone was valued at $1,250,000. In the open insurance market on the $5,000,000 at risk, three-quarters is held in London and the rest in Hamburg and Liverpool. The going rate before this tragedy was $3.75 per $500 at Lloyd's of London, where it jumped immediately to $300 per $500.

WHITE STAR AND *TITANIC*

The steerage or third class tickets were the bread and butter of the White Star Line. The success of the White Star passenger trade was because of them, for the Third Class paid the bills. Everything else was frosting on the cake—pure profit. Thus, it was very easy for White Star to splurge on the first three top decks which were 1st Class—the exquisite woodwork, the fabulously extravagant state rooms, the perfect quality of the silk hangings and the flooring, the fantastic chandeliers. Never before or ever since has a passenger ship been so lovely. Famous women in First Class were overheard saying how *Titanic* was better than anything they had ever seen in the fanciest of hotels in America and in Europe.

It is oft mentioned that *Titanic* was unsinkable. Actually, it was the words of two magazines, the *Ship Builder* and *Marine Engineer* who first coined the phrase that the ship was "Practically Unsinkable". The owners did not make that claim, although it became commonly overheard later on as everyone repeated it. It especially was thought by many to be tempting FATE and tempting the Gods. The Greatest Ship of the Ocean was completely outfitted in "State of the Art" safety features. No one could ever say that *Titanic* was delinquent in any of its responsibilities. It was completely legal concerning the regulations for life boats (enough for 1176 people). It was the largest steamship at that time. The owners certainly went beyond the call of duty in arranging the accommodations.

The best first class suites even had small private decks. The walls were covered in masterpieces by the best artists, and the carved woodwork was incomparable. The most beautiful of china and the finest quality of sheets and other linens were beyond top quality. The accommodations rivaled or surpassed that of the Ritz in London and Sherry's in New York. It was even nicer than the richest of rich in 1st Class had in their own mansions. The band played during dinner, the ladies in their pale pastels and clinging gauze, with the men in white tie. The elegant opulence included a telephone system, a large barber shop, a swimming pool, a lending library, and a gym and squash court. First Class had electric baths, and their common rooms were outfitted in fancy carved paneling and luxurious furniture. Their Café Parisian was an elegant verandah brightly lit by the sun, serving fine cuisine.

Second Class, like First Class, was furnished in a way designed to be a bit more elegant than they were used to, as was 3rd class. No one had any reason to complain. The menus were made appropriate for each. And yet each one was well-treated. No one was discriminated against, for the only way to discriminate between the three classes was the ticket they bought. There was very little leaving of their own areas once the ship went to sea. Everyone on the boat was served their meal on nice china. No buffet for any of the passengers. The Third Class general room was paneled in pine and outfitted with sturdy teak furniture.

Titanic had three electric lifts in First Class, and one in Second Class. Steam-driven generators provided the power for an extended electrical system including providing electric lights all over the ship and two Marconi radios.

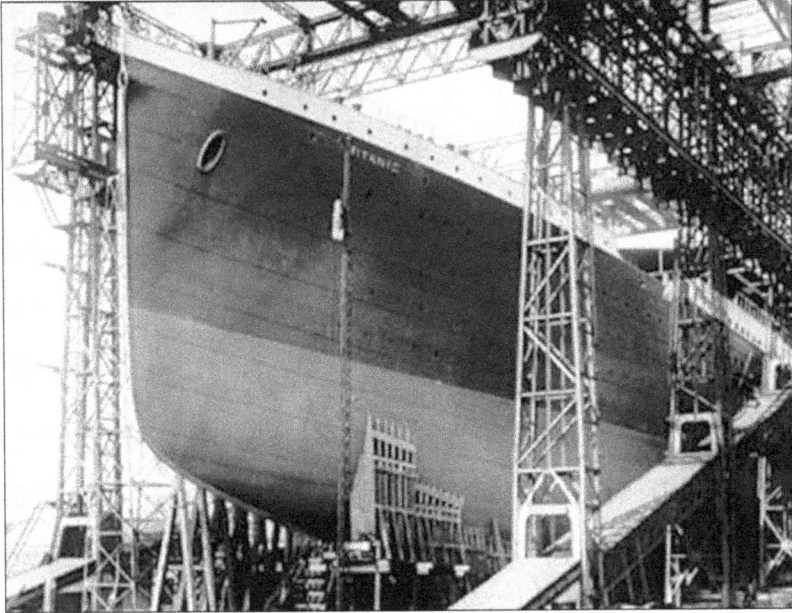

THE BUILDING OF *TITANIC*

The Good Ship *Titanic* took several years to build. At 882½ feet long, its length was more than the Washington Monument was tall. Ditto for the Grand Pyramid and St. Peters Church in Rome. The massive center anchor weighing 15½ tons took a 20-horse team to deliver.

The launching of *Titanic* was a movie miracle in the making. It took place in May of 1911. The next ten months were spent fitting her out. Just to get her off the scaffolding holding it back, it took train oil, some kind of soft soap, and tallow—some 23 tons of it. Once she started moving it took only 62 seconds to hit the water.

After the months of fitting out, and passing all of her tests with flying colors, the ship proceeded to Southampton where the excited crowds lined the walkways, looking at the famous and elegant passengers, just as much as the huge Ship of Dreams. Some records showed a head count of 2222 passengers.

Rushing along now to make up for time lost in a harbor incident with the ship *New York,* **Titanic** stopped only briefly that night at Cherbourg around 7 p.m. Everyone wanted to make this maiden voyage one for the record books, so any delay was more than tiresome.

It was here at Cherbourg that Bert Johns boarded the awesome **Titanic** along with several others he knew from Hardin, Lebanon. A load of mail was also put on board. The Syrians were coming to America for a new start. Some were joining family members; others would be looking for new jobs in America. They left with great anticipation for the upcoming voyage and the exciting new life in the United States and Canada.

Next brief stop was Queenstown harbor about noon where they took on a few additional passengers. These were immigrants coming to America from Ireland. Each man, woman and child boarding the massive launch must have felt a bit overwhelmed by the size.

As they took that first step onto the mighty **Titanic**, everyone, no matter who or what they were or had been—did anyone feel any tiny bit of FEAR? Any apprehension whatsoever? Surely no one taking that small first step on board the Great Ship gave any thought at all to any kind of maritime disaster or to any problems of any kind whatsoever.

The promenade deck

And so Bert Johns, a quiet young man just looking for a new start in America, came aboard the ship taking his first step to his ultimate DESTINY. Would he live or would he die? What part would FATE play in his Date with Death? Actually, his Fate was already sealed, along with every other person aboard. There would be no going back. Each passenger, steward, waiter, ships' officer, hired help, rich (total worth $250,000,000), engineer, cook, poor, old, young—they were all equals on that day. FATE was stepping in. All told, some sources say 1,635 men, women and children died that night. The American Inquiry gave 1,517, while the British Board of Trade settled on 1,490 total. Only 651 were destined to set foot on dry land again.

The poor, the blind, the deaf, the kind, the small, the large, the mean—everyone who took that same first step onto the deck of the wonderful Ship of Dreams, little did they know that their actions in the next few short days would ultimately determine their Destiny. Each and every one would have his own appointment with DEATH. Some said the ship was unsinkable, but sources say the first quote was "Only GOD can sink this ship." Others insist it was "Only GOD can save this ship." Every step each one took, every small decision made in the next four days would determine which would be their FATE—to live or to die.

CHRISTENING

When we think of the already-famous *Titanic* getting ready to slide into the sea for its maiden voyage, we can picture the christening, with a beautiful lady blessing the ship as she gently smashes the bow of the Queen of the Ocean with a bottle of bubbly champagne. Didn't happen. As a matter of fact, no one ever christened the super ship. A worker at the shipyards at that time said, "They just builds 'er and shoves 'er in".

Titanic left Belfast on April 2, 1912, a magnificent and spectacular sight to see . . . she was 50% larger than any other ships in service, excepting, of course, her sister ship, the *Olympic*. She weighed more than 46,000 tons.

PASSENGERS OF THE *RMS TITANIC* (Wikipedia)

Once again reports contradict each other. There was a lot of talk about passengers being divided into three separate classes. The price of the ticket determined the class, but to some it was a matter of social class.

The First Class consisted of the wealthiest passengers on board. They were prominent upper class citizens. They came from many different walks of life, including pro athletes, businessmen, bankers, high-ranking military men, industrialists. Most of these brought along their personal staff, which included chauffeurs, valets, nurses for the children, and maids.

The social elite of America were proud and excited to be on the maiden voyage of the Great *Titanic*. Millionaire Colonel John Jacob Astor IV and his 18-year old pregnant wife Madeleine were returning to the United States for their child's birth . . . Major Archibald Butt, who was President Taft's military aide, returning to resume his duties after a six-week trip to Europe . . . George D. Wick, founder and president of Youngstown Sheet and Tube . . . Charles Hays, president of Canada's Grand Trunk Railway . . . Denver millionaire and women's rights activist the Unsinkable Molly Brown . . . John Thayer, Pennsylvania Railroad Executive . . . American silent film Dorothy Gibson . . . industrialist Benjamin Guggenheim . . . Macy's Department Store Isidor Straus and wife Ida.

J.P. Morgan, who was a financier of White Star Line, and Milton S. Hershey, cancelled their trip on the Mighty *Titanic* at the last minute.

Professors, clergymen, tourists, authors were all middle-class passengers, although some chose Third Class tickets. A schoolteacher, Lawrence Beesley, who was a science master at Dulwich College, spent much of the trip in the library. He was a survivor. Two months after the sinking, he wrote and published *The Loss of the **SS TITANIC***, the first eyewitness account of the disaster.

A slightly scandalous Second Class French family was composed of two sons and their father, a French tailor, Michel Navratil, who travelled incognito under an alias of Louis M. Hoffman. He had kidnapped his own two boys from his estranged wife to take to the United States. The father died in the sinking. The boys became "The *Titanic* Orphans."

Third Class was almost all immigrants. Third Class passengers were made up of large numbers of Irish, British, & Scandinavians. Central and Eastern Europe, including Bulgaria, Croatia and Russia added their share. The Middle East, primarily Lebanon and Syria, and Hong Kong, and Armenians fleeing Turkey made up the rest.

TITANIC TIMELINE

July 29 1908   *Titanic* design was approved.

March 31 1909   Keel of *Titanic* laid.

May 31 1911   12 Noon   The ship's hull was successfully launched.

April 3 1912   *Titanic* arrives in Southampton.

April 10 1912   9:30-11:30   Passengers arrive and begin to board.

April 10 1912   Noon   *Titanic* begins her maiden voyage.

April 10 1912   6:30 pm   *Titanic* visits Cherbourg, France,
                             and picks up more passengers. Bert
                             Johns boarded with others he knew
                             from Hardin, Lebanon. The Great Ship
                             fascinated them all.

R.M.S. TITANIC.

APRIL 10, 1912.

HORS D'ŒUVRE VARIÉS

CONSOMMÉ RÉJANE   CRÈME REINE MARGOT

TURBOT, SAUCE HOMARD
WHITEBAIT

MUTTON CUTLETS & GREEN PEAS
SUPRÊME OF CHICKEN À LA STANLEY

SIRLOIN OF BEEF, CHÂTEAU POTATOES
ROAST DUCKLING, APPLE SAUCE
FILLET OF VEAL & BRAISED HAM

CAULIFLOWER   SPINACH
BOILED RICE
BOVIN & BOILED NEW POTATOES

PLOVER ON TOAST & CRESS
SALAD

PUDDING SANS SOUCI
CHARLOTTE COLVILLE
GRANVILLES

FRENCH ICE CREAM

** Bert Johns has less than 4 days to live or to die.

April 11 1912   11:30 am   The ship reached Queenstown, Ireland. Mail and more passengers were loaded on *Titanic*.

April 12 & 13   *Titanic* sailed through calm waters as the passengers prepared for the ride of their lives. The sea was a flat calm, no moon and clear skies filled with shooting stars.

** Bert Johns and the other passengers and crew were totally enjoying their trip on the Mighty *Titanic*. It was everything they had been told, everything they had imagined. The food was incomparable, the accommodations better than anything they had expected.

FOOD

Titanic carried 60 chefs: the soup chefs, the roast cooks, the pastry cooks, and vegetable cooks, and a kosher cook. On Saturday and Sunday there were 36 glass men and plate washers, scullery men. They prepared over 6,000 meals a day.

How much food? Well—according to Walter Lord's <u>A Night to Remember</u>:

75,000 pounds of fresh meat

11,000 pounds of fresh fish

7500 pounds of bacon and ham

2200 pounds of coffee

800 pounds of tea

40,000 fresh eggs

2500 pounds of sausages

1000 pounds of sweetbreads (calves' organs)

10,000 pounds of sugar

200 barrels of flour

1000 pounds of grapes

36,000 oranges

16,000 lemons

1500 gallons fresh milk

3500 pounds of onions

7000 heads of lettuce

40 Tons of potatoes

1750 quarts of Ice cream

1200 quarts of fresh cream

6000 pounds of fresh butter

50 boxes of grapefruit

2¾ Tons of tomatoes

1120 pounds of marmalades and jams

800 bundles of fresh asparagus

2250 pounds of fresh green peas

A Third Class menu for breakfast included: oatmeal porridge, smoked herring, jacket potatoes, tripe (part of cow's stomach) and onions, and Swedish bread and marmalade.

ENTERTAINMENT AND MORE

Besides having terrific food, the glorious *Titanic* was well equipped for FUN. In First Class you could go swimming in fresh sea water in the pool for 25 cents. *Titanic* and her sister ship, *Olympic,* were apparently among the first to install swimming pools. The men in First Class could swim for free, 6 am until 9 am. A squash court was available for 50 cents, which included a professional instructor. They could exercise in the gym. Turkish baths were open to the men from 2:00 pm until 6:00 pm, while the First Class women could use them any day from 10:00 am until 1:00 pm. There was a nice darkroom on A-Deck where pictures could be developed. Or passengers could luxuriate lying in the fabulous deck chairs, nicely covered for their convenience with blankets emblazoned with the White Star logos, while hot drinks were being served. The chairs and blankets could be rented for $1.00.

Fun activities for Second Class included socializing in the library, or the men could go into the smoking room. They could play dominoes or chess, or walk the deck. They could also use the deck chairs.

Steerage (or Third Class) was the least expensive ticket, and that provided for the men a general room for smoking and playing cards. Instruments could be played and anyone could dance. They could, of course, walk the deck and sit on benches on the poop deck, which was the highest outdoor deck on the stern. Steerage was near the rudder in the stern or steering equipment. But it did have two bathtubs!

Hospitals? Of course. If you were sick there were two doctors on board ship.

Titanic's gymnasium on the Boat Deck, which was equipped with the latest exercise machines. (Wikipedia)

April 14

Throughout the day ice warnings kept arriving. The sunset was beautiful, but most had stayed inside after lunch because of the drop in temperature, which remained hovering around 31 or 32 degrees. It was cold enough that very few passengers took more than a quick look at the beautiful skies that night. The water was dark and looked like obsidian, combining with the gorgeous sunset to make a picture-perfect sight.

April 14   11:40 pm

Lookout Fleet spotted an iceberg dead ahead which hit the starboard side. They had no binoculars.

April 14   11:50 pm

Water had poured in and risen 14 feet in the front of the mighty *Titanic*.

April 15   12:00 am

The Captain was told the ship could stay afloat a couple of hours. The calls for HELP went out.

Meanwhile, Bert Johns had become separated from his friends in all the confusion. The pushing and shoving and screaming all around him was awful, and he saw no one he knew. The ship officials were shouting, "Stop. Get back. Women and children only." He didn't know what they were saying. He didn't understand any of it. He didn't speak a word of English. It was getting down to that final decision that he and every person aboard ship would have to make . . . would you live or would you die? The story of Bert Johns' courageous decision has been a *Titanic* mystery.

As the boat sank, the other Syrians left on board did an amazing thing—instead of acting like fools, pushing and shoving and carrying on because they knew they were about to die, these stalwart Syrians accepted their Fate. They took out their musical instruments and began to play until the ship disappeared from sight. One took a wooden flute (Mijwiz) while the others were standing shoulder to shoulder and began to stamp their feet and sing. Some say the Armenians were treated very badly by some of the ship's officers—that they were prevented from boarding any lifeboats, and that they were actually singled out to be shot. Unfortunately, there appears to be some truth in that. (See: The Dream and then the Nightmare—The Syrians who boarded the *Titanic*).

The massive ship now sits 12,460 feet down at the bottom of the sea. And yes, husbands and wives, little children lost their lives. And it was sad when the Great Ship went down.

George Jacub reviewed <u>The Dream and Then the Nightmare for the "Titanic Review"</u> in July 2011.

In his review he stated: "(For the purpose of this book, Syrian means residents of the former Ottoman Empire —

Syrians, Lebanese, Armenians — before the Middle East was divided into the countries we now know.)"

THE THREE DAYS, APRIL 11, 12, 13—

TITANIC ICEBERG MESSAGES & FACTS

Messages from other vessels, like the *SS Californian* (which was only five miles away at the time of the disaster) kept coming in all day sending messages of congratulations and by the way, look for icebergs. Nobody gave the icebergs any thought at all, except as a beautiful sight to see.

SS *Californian*, which had tried to warn *Titanic* of the danger from pack-ice
(Wikipedia)

TITANIC BY THE NUMBERS

There were 710 tickets sold in Steerage. Remember, the Third Class tickets provided the bread and butter of *Titanic*. It paid for the costs. A ticket for Third Class, berth ticket, was $35.00.

Second Class held 285 passengers. Their tickets cost $65.00.

There were 329 spaces available in First Class. $430.00 was the cost of a First Class ticket. There were also two deluxe parlor suites.

The crew members totaled 892.

The total, not counting crew, was 1324 passengers, although these numbers vary according to whom you were talking to.

Total Cost to build: $7.5 million.

Shipyard workers earned $10.00 a week.

Titanic had 200 miles of electric cable and 2000 windows and portholes.

Size: 4 city blocks or 882½ feet long, wide as a four-lane highway (92½ feet), as tall as an 11 story building.

Weight was 53,000 Tons.

CARGO ON *TITANIC*:

Thousands of Tons of coal

One Renault car

Fifteen huge cranes and winches

Two cases of grandfather clocks

Olive oil—25 cases

76 cases of dragon's blood

(sap from palm trees in Canary Islands, used to color wood varnishes)

Women's make-up

Ostrich plumes—12 cases

Shelled Walnuts—300 cases

Straw hats—4 cases

Champagne—63 cases

Hairnets—4 packages

Potatoes—1,196 bags

Mercury—2 barrels

Rough oak beams

THE WRECK AND SINKING OF *TITANIC*

After the iceberg hit the boat, most passengers were almost completely unconcerned. It was a cold night outside of their rooms, so most went back to bed. Few recognized any danger. Why would they? This was *Titanic*, the Ship of Dreams, the Gem of the Ocean. She was unsinkable. And then the water starting coming in. The lifeboats were being readied to launch. A lot of trouble occurred when the lifeboats on the starboard side were lowered and capsized. On the port side away from the iceberg, the boats were lowering safely. Many different versions leading up to the sinking and the next hours following have been reported. Nothing of a panic occurred, at least in some people's minds—while stories of complete and utter horrid behavior were also reported.

It was over a half hour from the time the iceberg hit that the boats were starting to fill. As the ship started to sink, many of the people got to their knees to pray. Many had gone back to their staterooms.

Major Arthur G. Peuchen of Toronto—*NEWARK NEWS*

According to the staff correspondent of the Newark Star reporting on April 24, 1912, during the Senate Committee hearings investigating the terrible tragedy and sinking of *Titanic*, Major Arthur Peuchen of Toronto, a voluntary witness, made some startling accusations about Quartermaster Hichen. He branded him as a coward. He insisted that Hichen was directly responsible for the loss of about forty people. He left *Titanic* with only 23 passengers in a lifeboat. Despite being signaled from the sinking boat to return to pick up more passengers and to save struggling victims in the water, Quartermaster Hichen did not respond except to keep going away from the sinking boat. He was accused of ignoring the prayers and tears of the women in the lifeboat with him, and he continued on when he could have and should have filled his boat to full capacity. Major Peuchen labeled him a dirty coward.

"The Quartermaster imagined he saw a light ahead. I could not, although I have a good deal of sea experience. He thought the light might be on a buoy and called out to another boat to ask if that were so. It seemed to me utterly absurd to look for a buoy in that part of the Atlantic. The whistle was evidently sounded for us when the last boats were being sent off and it was evident to the Captain and the officers that *Titanic* could not float much longer. The whistling ceased. There was a rumbling sound. The lights on the steamer went out. Then there was a series of explosions, dreadful calls and cries, which deeply affected the women in the lifeboat. The cries were horrible to listen to. They became fainter and fainter, then died out.

"We did not see *Titanic* sink. We could not see her after the lights went out. We were five-eighths of a mile away from her."

"From what you observed was there proper discipline on that part of the crew in the loading of the lifeboats?" asked a Senator.

"Those of crew I saw working preserved good discipline, but the number was too few. I can't speak for the whole boat, but the crew were too few on the port side. I was surprised that there were not more sailors. I was surprised that there were not more persons loaded into the boats. Our lifeboat was lashed to another boat after being adrift several hours. That boat spared us a man to help row.

"How many persons, all told, were there in the boats that you helped to load?"

"Thirty-six or thirty-seven in one, and twenty-three in the other. These two boats alone could have carried seventy more persons"

S.O.S.

THE SIGNAL THAT FLASHES NEWS OF DISASTER THROUGH THE AIR

NEWARK NEWS Report

When *Titanic* was still hundreds of miles out to sea, the wireless lines were abuzz with the brand-new "mystic and magic S.O.S." worldwide cry of distress on the ocean. From the time the Queen of the Ocean's antennae went out, "Three dots, three dashes, three dots" in the international code of American Morse Code, S.O.S. was here to say HELP! The old code was still in use, 'C.Q.D.', by which Jack Binns saved the people on the *Republic*. Apparently the old code 'C.Q.D.' had been preferred; however, it was too common and faked by hundreds of amateurs.

When the now-famous S.O.S. is sent out, every ship in range receiving the signal within hundreds of miles drops everything and heads for the location of the distressed ship immediately. Over and over again the three simple, short letters, S.O.S.—no other meaningful message—similar to a stock market ticker going in another room far distant, is faintly heard through the receiving operator headgear. Then the message is relayed on and on to every ship within range, asking for help.

On the night of April 14, with the mighty *Titanic* fading fast, the operator of the sinking ship signals to the officers' bridge of the ship they hope can reach them in time. Ditto the signal goes to the engine room. By that time, the forced draught hits the engines, and every ounce of speed, and every possible turn of the propellers is forced from them. THE RACE TO SAVE NEARLY 3000 LIVES IS ON!

The *Virginian* was able to turn around to come to the aid of **Titanic** after receiving this call on the wireless, "Sinking by the head, and women are being rushed in to the lifeboats." That was the last word to the *Virginian* from the mighty **Titanic**. The *Carpathia* beat them there.

The antennae of the giant liner flashed the S.O.S. all through the night until the wires became silent—every wireless operator within range of the maimed ship tried to locate her. Only the three fatal letters, S.O.S. kept going on, over and over, their world-wide cry of distress. For **Titanic** it was too late.

FOG OR NO FOG?

From *NEWARK NEWS*

The Newark papers did a tremendous job in covering the horror story of the mighty ocean liner, filled with thousands of people and workers. "No FOG When Monster of the Sea Struck *Titanic*. The collision occurred in latitude 41.46 north and longitude 50.14 west, 1,150 miles east of Newfoundland. Contrary to early surmises, there was NO FOG to hinder sight of the Gem of the Ocean. The weather was clear and the water a deadly calm. Almost as soon as the *Virginian* picked up the distress signal it was recorded by the operator of *Titanic's* sister ship and next to her the largest vessel afloat. This was at midnight. At that hour she was 200 miles from New York en route to Southampton. The *Olympic* forged ahead under full steam but tonight's wireless dispatches indicate she was too late to be of any assistance. The *Baltic*, famous for her rescue of the passengers of the steamer *Republic,* was the next ship to get the brief story of the Great Ship's plight. She was on her way from New York to Liverpool but turned on full speed toward *Titanic's* position. The *Parisian,* according to her messages, reached the flotilla of rescuers shortly after the *Baltic's* message from Captain Haddock tonight confirmed the fears of the White Star Line officials that the women and children who escaped in the small boats from the $10,000,000 ship had perished.

A part of the message was withheld, but enough was divulged to the newspapers to make certain the appalling extent of the tragedy. Not until Captain Haddock flashed, "Horrible disaster—all but 670 lost," would the White Star admit that the mightiest ship ever launched had gone down on her maiden voyage.

"The scene in the White Star offices tonight was pitiful. Brought to the realization of the complete destruction of the fruit of their dreams—gray-haired men, many of them veteran seamen themselves, were distraught.

"Vice-President P.A.S. Franklin, of the White Star Line, said tonight, 'We have heard the rumor from Halifax that three steamers—the *Virginian*, *Parisian,* and *Carpathia* are heading for the **Titanic's** position. We have received a wireless from Captain Haddock of the *Olympic*, that the **Titanic** sunk at 2:20 am. We have also heard indirectly that the *Carpathia* has 675 survivors aboard. The **Titanic** passenger list numbered 2,000. It is difficult to say whether the *Virginian* and the *Parisian* have any survivors aboard until we get a direct report.

The *Carpathia* is proceeding direct to New York. We very much fear there has been a serious loss of life, but it is impossible at this time to assure ourselves that the other steamers have or have not survivors aboard.

TITANIC WAS WORLD'S LARGEST SHIP

FLOATING PALACE THOUGHT UNSINKABLE

The Newark Newspaper provided a thorough presentation of the Floating Palace we call *Titanic*. She weighed nearly 1,000 tons greater than her sister ship *Olympic*, and displaced 66,000 tons. Not only was she a floating marvel of luxury, she carried literally a town full of people. She was 15 stories high. *Titanic* had three propellers. The outer or wing ones were turned by reciprocating engines and the middle propeller by a steam turbine.

Each stateroom had its own tub, with all kinds of water. The maids, servants and valets had their own servants' hall. There was an old English chop-house with high-backed stalls of black oak. The arbors combined real flowers with fake vines, making a spectacular sight. Sitting rooms were 15 X 15 feet.

The New White Star Liner,
R.M.S. "TITANIC"

VINOLIA OTTO TOILET SOAP

In the double bottom alone there were 500,000 rivets, 1¾ inches in diameter, and weighing 270 Tons. The plates in the bottom were 36 feet long and weighed 4¼ Tons each. The largest beam in her was 92 feet long and weighed more than four Tons. The frame of the stern weighed 70 Tons; the rudder 100 Tons; the boss arms 73½ Tons aft and 40 Tons forward. Three million steel rivets were used in binding her massive plates, which weighed 1,200 Tons. The vessel had nine steel decks.

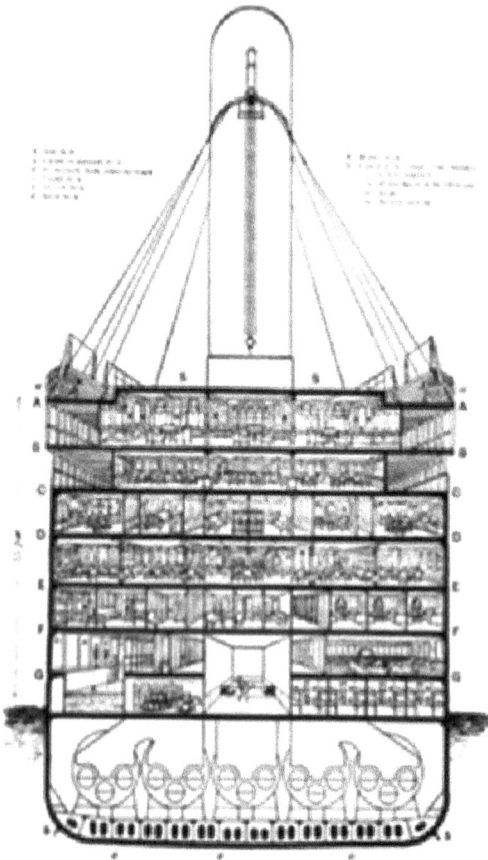

Cutaway diagram of *Titanic's* midship section (Wikipedia)

TEN FOOT GATE

From the *Chicago American*, Friday, April 26, 1912: An eyewitness aboard the Ship of Dreams refuted the claims made by others that a gate was not locked to prevent Third Class passengers from getting to the lifeboats.

Lynn, Mass., April 25—TEN FOOT GATE HELD *TITANIC* STEERAGE FOLES IN DEATH TRAP:

"A ten-foot high gate was locked, making prisoners of the Third Class cabin people on the ship." This according to Miss Annie Jermyn, twenty-two years old. She went on to say that it took her two hours to get over the gate, which barred the only exit. Nobody asked her to get into a boat, she asserts, although she stood on the deck near the davits in her night dress and bare feet.

She went on to say, "The last boat was about to start from the ship with only about fifteen aboard. Realizing that it was my only chance, I sprang from the upper deck of the vessel into the boat, falling nearly thirty feet and landing on my chest. A second later a man fell beside me, but he had no sooner got up and taken a seat in the boat than an officer drew his revolver and shot him in the head. I fainted as they pitched the lifeless body of the poor fellow into the sea."

PANIC (*TITANIC* Historical Society)

(*Chicago Daily Journal*, April 19)

Mrs. Hippach's account of the tragedy report: "As they were being swung over the side Mrs. Hippach said she saw the first evidence of panic. Some of the men attempted to crowd the women away from the rail, but were driven back by Major Butt and other Americans and Englishmen.

RECOVERING THE DEAD—Wikipedia

Of the 711 passengers and crew rescued by the *Carpathia*, six had succumbed either in a lifeboat or on the rescue ship the next morning and were buried at sea.

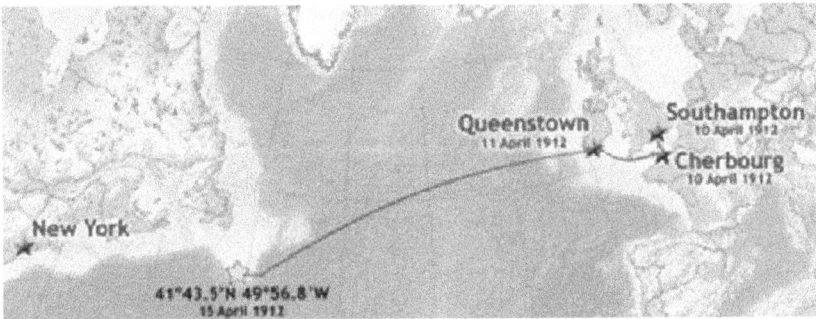

Several ships sailed to the spot of the sinking of **Titanic** to help in the recovery of victim's bodies. White Star chartered the cable ship *CS Mackay-Bennett* from Halifax, Nova Scotia, to search out and pick up any deceased. Three other ships followed in the search: the sealing ship *Algerine*, the lighthouse supply ship *Montmagny* and the cable ship *Minia*. Each ship carried embalming supplies, clergy, and undertakers. Apparently, each body recovered had to be embalmed before returning to port. It was the law of the sea, or so it was said. Every cadaver was numbered and given a detailed description to help identify it . . . height, weight, hair and eye color, age, visible birthmarks, tattoos. Each body was catalogued and personal effects marked and placed in canvas bags corresponding to their number.

Unfortunately, the embalming supplies on the ships were soon gone, because there were so many bodies. Captain Larnder of the *Mackay-Bennett* and the undertakers aboard decided to preserve all bodies of First Class passengers, justifying their decision by the need to visually identify wealthy men to resolve any disputes over large estates. Consequently, most of the burials at sea were crew and Third Class passengers.

Colonel Archibald Gracie . . . a Survivor's Story

" . . . the agonizing cries of death from over a thousand throats, the wails and groans of the suffering, the shrieks of the terror-stricken and the awful gasping for breath of those in the last throes of drowning, none of us will ever forget until our dying day: "Help! Help! Boat ahoy! Boat ahoy!" And "My God! My God!" were the heartrending cries and shrieks of men, which floated to us over the surface of the dark waters continuously for the next hour, but as time went on, growing weaker and weaker until they died out entirely.

C.E.H. Stengel TELLS STORY OF HIS RESCUE

NEWARK NEWS

The sinking of *Titanic*, the struggle of her passengers to save themselves from an awful death and the rescue by the *Carpathia* was graphically told by C.E. Henry Stengel, an eyewitness, who with his wife was picked up by the *Carpathia*, to a Star reporter on the way from the Cunard pier to the Lincoln Park home of Mr. and Mrs. Stengel last night. His story begins with the time when *Titanic* struck the huge iceberg until the time her passengers were taken aboard by the *Carpathia*.

"There were not enough boats to care for the passengers. None but the captain was aware of the danger after striking the iceberg. Many men preferred to remain aboard the *Titanic* rather than chance it in the lifeboats. The crew was inadequate, being composed of a strange set of men. Mr. Stengel declared that an officer of *Titanic* told him on board the *Carpathia* that it had been figured out on the ill-fated vessel that it would encounter icebergs between 10 and 12 o'clock Sunday night. Mr. Stengel is willing to take an affidavit to this effect.

"*Titanic* struck the berg at 11:40 and sunk at 2:20. The water at this time was perfectly calm and as smooth as glass. It was so cold, however, that the ship's doctors declared that no one could live in it more than twenty minutes. Of the passengers saved, according to Mr. Stengel there were 199 crew, 136 Third Class, 115 Second Class, and 210 First Class.

CENSORSHIP ON PRESS DISPATCHES

Survivor C.E.H. Stengel commented on the lack of truthful press dispatches:

Authorities on the *Carpathia* insisted that only twenty words of press could be sent each day . . . *that is, only twenty words sent a day!*

Only three couples on board **Titanic** who were separated on the ship were reunited. Mr. and Mrs. Stengel were one of those. She was lowered into a lifeboat soon after the first crash. "After Mrs. Stengel had been lowered I walked up toward the bow and saw them preparing to lower the lifeboats, on which I finally put out to sea." He was somehow permitted to take a seat in a lifeboat much later. Somehow Mr. Stengel was the first person to reach the *Carpathia*, not fully dressed, while Mrs. Stengel only wore a kimono over her nightdress.

The report from the Newark papers related that the lifeboat he was saved in was occupied by four other persons not counting himself . . . Sir and Lady Cosmo Duff Gordon, a Miss Francacelle and A.L. Sullivan, of New York. (Could it be possible, only five in one boat?)

The boat they were in was afloat for over four hours, Mr. Stengel helping to man the craft. His hands were so numb that he had to be lifted aboard the rescue liner by ropes. He made it very clear that the ship officers on **Titanic** were prepared to shoot any man from trying to get into a lifeboat. The Law of the Sea at that time was "Women and Children first".

"I wish you to emphatically say that Colonel John Jacob Astor was not threatened by any of the officers. The last seen of him he was calmly walking the upper deck.

CAPTAIN ENTERTAINING, BUT NOT DRINKING—MR. STENGEL'S STORY CONTINUED

"I hardly know where to begin. As I sit here now I can still hear the wailing and moaning of the 1,500 or more persons who jumped into the sea after the four explosions that took place on the *Titanic*.

"The ship that we thought unsinkable, the ship that men stuck to rather than take a chance in the lifeboats, sank in less than three hours—to be exact in two hours and forty minutes. At this time I can but thank GOD that my wife and I are here, and that we can once more clasp our near and dear ones in our arms.

"Let me begin at the beginning . . .

"We retired about 10 o'clock. We had attended the concert and we knew that the captain was entertaining and dining his friends, among whom was Bruce Ismay, until 10 o'clock. Please say for me, in justice to Captain Smith, that he had not been drinking. He smoked cigarettes, but he did not drink.

"I had been sleeping but a short time and was having a terrible dream which I cannot fully remember when I felt a shock. This was no greater than one caused by the propeller coming above the surface of the water. I thought, nevertheless, that I would go on deck and ascertain if there was any trouble. There I found but few persons. No one seemed to fear danger. The first inkling that I had of danger was when I saw the serious face of Captain Smith as he talked to George Widener of Philadelphia.

"The first order was to put on the life preservers and to prepare the boats—this merely as a precaution. Even then it was not thought that it would be necessary to use either. This was about midnight. I cannot repeat too often that we thought the ship absolutely unsinkable. When we struck the iceberg the portholes were open and some of the ice jammed through into the staterooms. One of the men picked up the ice and as he held it in his hand said smilingly, 'We must have struck an iceberg.' He had absolutely no thought of making any preparations to leave the ship.

"***Titanic*** struck on her starboard side and her sides were ripped open where the coal bunkers are located. On the starboard side there were about six boats lowered. I do not know much about the other side. The women were put immediately into the boats. The wives were separated from their husbands, daughters from their fathers. Mrs. Isidor Straus, rather than be separated from her husband, chose to die with him.

NO PLUGS IN TWO OF THE BOATS

Mr. Stengel continued, "Another indication of the negligence of the steamship company was that two of the boats had no plugs in them when they were lowered. These boats are believed to be lost. There was no food, no light, no compass and no water in any of the boats. We just trusted to GOD. My boat met with difficulty right at the start. Its painter was stuck fast and it was only after considerable time had been spent that she was finally loosened and lowered.

"Some of the men ordered to man the boats proved themselves cowards. One Armenian wrapped himself in a blanket and refused absolutely to pull an oar. This boat was manned by two girls."

"A lane of sorrowing humanity packed the pier" as the survivors walked down the gangplank from the *Carpathia*. Every ear strained to catch those first words of the survivors. "The first words of most of those who were not too ill to talk were in the form of thanks to the Almighty at once more feeling land beneath their feet. Then in jerky sentences they tried to tell of the scenes of horror when *Titanic* struck . . ."

"The Misses Caroline and Lilly Bonnell of Youngstown said, 'We immediately rushed on deck, only stopping to throw on a coat over our night dresses. The night was bright and starlit.'"

"The last edition of the *Newark Star Morning* went to press only two hours after the gigantic liner struck the iceberg and began flashing its calls for assistance. The *Star* built up a story that was as complete in essential details, and decidedly more accurate that those contained in the last editions of yesterday's evening papers."

The *Star* also published the first list of the prominent persons aboard. In the final editions of all of yesterday's evening newspapers the viewpoint was decidedly optimistic—the authentic death tolls gave way to "all on board saved".

The facts were that the big ship was disabled, and its passengers were in terrible danger.

At 8:15 pm on April 15, the White Star officials began to admit that some people had died, refusing to give any estimate of the loss of life. Before that, the White Star officials had buried their necks in the sand, refusing to admit that the Queen of the Water, their Mighty **Titanic** had slipped below the water to the bottom of the sea, making it no doubt the most horrifying sea tale ever. Soon afterwards the White Star had good reason to issue this statement: "Our advices from the vicinity of the ill-fated **Titanic** indicate that there has been a horrible loss of life. We cannot estimate the number of lives lost at this hour."

TURN DOWN A GLASS FOR ME—FUTRELLE

This story was from Atlanta, GA. on April 17.

"Turn down a glass for me," was the last written message novelist Jacques Futrelle sent from Europe to a friend in Atlanta. Hugh Cordosa received the following not a few days before Futrelle sailed: "Been all over Italy, Austria, Germany and France. Sail for home soon. Turn down a glass for me." "FUTRELLE"

"Futrelle had a premonition of tragedy two weeks before he and his wife sailed. They took the precaution of sending from London to Mrs. Futrelle's brother, John Peele, of Atlanta, powers of attorney for the administration of their estates should anything befall them. Directions were also given as to the future care of their children. The novelist sent a list of the banking houses where he had his money and securities.

"You never can tell what will happen," the novelist wrote. "May and I want everything straight for the kiddies if anything should happen."

DROWNING OF ASTOR SHOCK TO SOCIETY

Hard for Fashionables to Realize that Plutocrat Shared Fate of Servant

New York, April 17:

"It was hard for society people to realize at first that a man said to possess as much as $150,000,000. had choked and struggled in the grip of the same fate that overtook the servant who had served him at dinner.

"Mrs. John Jacob Astor and "maid" were the only mention of their famous name in the list of survivors from the wrecked liner. Society people began to wonder about what it all means—when the first shock of the death of one of their most prominent leaders had passed.

"Kudos given for the Commander of *Titanic* as reports came in that Captain E.J. Smith stayed with the ship as it sunk. Many reported that he was last seen standing on the bridge as the great hulk plunged into the deep. The rescued passengers tell a thrilling story of the Captain's last stand in his position of command, fully realizing that his ship was lost and calmly waiting for the last moment."

SAYS CAPTAIN SHOT STEERAGE PASSENGERS

In a total contradiction of the above report, the *Chicago Daily Journal*, Thursday, April 24, 1912, in an Associated Press Telegram:

(Ottawa, Ontario)—Mrs. Mariana Assaf, a **Titanic** survivor, told friends here today that she saw several steerage passengers attempt to rush the lifeboats and that Capt. Smith shot down several of them: "Three cousins of mine pleaded for a seat, but were refused," she said.

TELLS HOW 100 DIED IN LIFEBOATS

Chicago American, Monday, April 22, 1912—

From the report of Mrs. Collyer as told by Mr. M.E. Smith, manager of the Chicago house of the Waterman Pen Company, who met Mrs. Harvey Collyer, a rescued passenger, in New York. She had gone through the night of horrors, and told her story of the strange experiences she encountered while she and her eight-year-old daughter, Margaret, were rescued. Mr. Collyer died on ***Titanic***.

"Nearly a hundred, Mrs. Collyer said, were drowned when lifeboats collapsed. Two or three others, she declared, were shot to death by the ship's officers in averting a stampede." Mrs. Collyer's story as told to Mr. Smith: "We were in the second cabin. There was a great rush for the boats after the alarm spread. I was pushed into a boat by my husband. He bid me goodbye. 'I'll join you in a later boat,' he said. He kissed me and the baby and that was the last I saw of him.

"While our boat was pulling away from the sinking ship two lifeboats were overturned. There were not less than ninety or a hundred persons in these two boats, some were women. Not a soul of these escaped. The boats, crowded to the limit, simply spilled into the sea. The oarsmen seemed to have lost their heads. There was a stampede on the ship. The scenes of panic were awful. The officers drew revolvers and waved the crowd back.

SAW THEM SHOT TO DEATH

"At last they had to fire. I covered my eyes as I sat in the lifeboat. Even then I saw them fall. I know they were shot to death.

"More than a dozen people jumped over the rail into the sea and were drowned, while others were being taken off in the lifeboats. The steerage crowds were crazed.

The *Newark News* Morning edition on Tuesday, April 16, 1912,

"1,800 PERISH AS GREAT SHIP GOES DOWN TO OCEAN BOTTOM"

"Property Loss So Colossal Figures Scarcely can convey it"

It is difficult to imagine how words can even begin to describe the horrendous news of the sinking of the world's largest ocean steamship. Eighteen hundred persons lost their lives at 2:30 o'clock on the morning of April 15, 450 miles east of Cape Race. "In addition to the great loss of life the property loss is so stupendous that figures scarcely can convey it to the human mind. The ship alone cost more than $10,000,000. More than five million in diamonds and bonds belonging to the passengers were locked in the vessel's safe.

REPORT OF THE CROW'S NEST OFFICERS

When questioned about the sighting of the iceberg at night, one man told the investigators that some men can see farther than others. He also responded directly to this question: Would glasses have added much to the range of vision? To which he replied, "I believe they would have."

Fleet, the lookout, told the investigators that when he sighted the iceberg he rang the 'three bells' danger signal and telephoned the bridge. There is a telephone in the crow's nest for that. <u>They had no spyglass.</u>

MOMENTS OF TERROR

A very interesting story was told by the Newark newspapers from the questioning in the Senate hearings. Telling of when the ship struck and was stopped by the terrifying pounding of her engines, Capt. Smith ordered all hands on deck. That all did not answer the summons was because many of those occupying forward cabins were killed by the impact.

The Senators also heard from one of the seamen in the Crow's-Nest at the time of the iceberg accident. Stunning news related that they were not outfitted with binoculars or spy glasses of any kind for long range, which consequently made it very difficult to see any distance ahead of the boat, and that he did not see the ice until it was too late.

Also from the Newark papers on that day, April 24, 1912, the headlines were shocking as they proclaimed, "IDENTIFY 42 BODIES OF THE 77 PICKED UP". "Name of Colonel John Jacob Astor Not in the List Received". "Butt may be one of them." "Representatives of Twenty Families Leave for Halifax to Claim their Dead." The article from New York dated April 23, 1912, related that White Star Line officials announced that the *Mackay-Bennett* cable ship picked up forty-two bodies of "verified dead", while a total of seventy-seven dead passengers were reported over the wireless.

"*TITANIC's* OFFICER TELLS OF HORRORS"
—New York, April 18

"Crew Ordered to Give First Cabin Passengers Preference for Lifeboats"

Joseph Boxhall, fourth officer of *Titanic*, who was in command of one of the lifeboats, made the following statement tonight:

"I was in bed when the crash came, but every officer and member of the crew leaped into his clothes as rapidly as possible and made the deck. The order was immediately given to get the lifeboats ready and awaken the passengers and get them to the deck.

"We were also ordered to give the preference to first-class passengers in filling the boats."

"The night was a bright one with the heavens studded with stars and the scene of the great commotion among the passengers was plainly visible all over the decks. Violence had to be used in some cases and numerous men were clubbed to the decks. When men tried to trample the women and children they were sent reeling to the deck and others in their mad scramble went over the sides without even a life preserver to cling to.

"I had sixteen souls in my boat, two of whom died before we were picked up by the *Carpathia*. Eleven were women and five were men.

"The last I saw of Capt. Smith he was on the bridge with the water reaching to his waist. We made our way through lanes of dead bodies and several of the boats were overturned by those in the water attempting to get aboard. The ship seemed to sink very slowly, and I should imagine two hours elapsed before it was out of sight. There was apparently but little suction.

THE MOST AWFUL OF SEA TRAGEDIES—*Newark Star* on Tuesday

An awful summation of *Titanic* tragedy was made by the Newark Star. It is printed in its entirety here:

"Hurling herself against an iceberg *Titanic* has gone down like a mammoth steel coffin, with more than 1500 of her passengers and crew. It is the most appalling tragedy in the history of the sea. Nothing approaching this loss of life has ever been recorded in the annals of the merchant marine. No detail is lacking to lend picturesque horror to the story that appalls civilization. This was the largest vessel ever built. She was on her maiden voyage. She represented an outlay of $10,000,000 and was the last word in modern comfort and luxury. These are details that add singularity to the stupendous disaster, but nothing to its horror and anguish. It touches hundreds of homes, the palace and the hovel. One circumstance softens the world-wide woe. There appears to have been the same chivalrous heroism that characterizes officers and crews of other British ships under similar circumstances. "Women and the Children first" was the word in that hour of death. These were put first into the boats and made up the greater part of the 670 saved out of a total of 2,200 souls, the officers and crew numbered 860. The calamity, too, is exceptional in the personnel of the probable victims. No such array of men powerful in the financial world, leaders in the aristocracy of society and the higher aristocracy of brains, ever figured on the passenger list of a lost steamship. Millionaire and day laborer, delicately nurtured dame and serving maid, philanthropist and immigrant, eminent scholar and illiterate peasant, all mingled in the leveling democracy of death. What scenes of frenzied anguish and silent resignation, mad terror and dauntless courage, were enacted in those last hours may be imagined—perhaps never be told.

SAYS LIFEBOATS PROVIDED WITH HARDTACK AND WATER.

It seems that there was a lot of confusion regarding preparedness of the lifeboats. The owners of the White Star Lines were concerned with all the rumors being spread. The Senate hearing found the Senators questioning this extensively. Apparently, there was hardtack and fresh water on them. There was also a light in the described lifeboat. These things were checked after the survivors went onto the *Carpathia*. There was an almost supreme confidence in the officers and crew that ***Titanic*** was unsinkable. A lot of time was wasted in believing this instead of getting the passengers and the lifeboats going. Comments like this from Mr. Hays: "This boat is good for eight hours yet, and by that time there will be assistance here." were reported at the Senators' query. There was no general alarm to the passengers. Two women narrowly escaped being drowned in their quarters. They were next door to the Astors. Mrs. Astor awakened them when she realized their danger.

Madeleine Astor

TITANIC DISASTER DEPRESSES STOCKS

Nothing of Importance Is Attempted in the
Market as a Result

New York, April 18

Reports out of New York on April 18 were not surprising, as the whole country stood back and recoiled from the Luxury Cruise Disaster.

"The opening was strong with high records in New York, Central, Bethlehem Steel, Beet Sugar and Wabash 4%, bonds, Steel rose a point and all issues showed material advance over the closing of the previous day. The trading was light and prices gradually worked an average of nearly a point lower from sheer inertia."

A very disappointing rate of dividend at 4 per cent by the Amalgamated directors, compared with what the rate of 2 per cent had been for years. They were hoping for 5 per cent. That stock dropped one-half point when it was announced.

STOCK EXCHANGE MEMBERS RAISE $20,000.
FOR SUFFERERS FROM WRECK

The Stock Exchange President, R. H. Thomas, met the survivors of *Titanic* disaster at the docking of the *Carpathia* with $20,000. It went to the survivors of the ship sinking who had no one there to meet them at the dock. Willing guides stepped up to assist them in finding a place to go.

COFFINS

Pier 53's floor was rapidly becoming filled with rows and rows of coffins, which did absolutely nothing to encourage the people waiting impatiently for the *Carpathia* to show up.

The Stephen Merritt Cremation Company brought the equivalent of a carload. The grim boxes were trucked in on a long procession of wagons. P.W. Radcliffe, Vice-President of the company, told this story: he had been ordered to have every available coffin delivered to the pier by 11:00, and he was following directions implicitly.

When pressured by the newspapermen regarding numbers of casualties, he could not respond. It seems that both the *Cunard* and *White Star Lines* officials had simply told him that all the coffins he could get would be needed. Frank E. Campbell, undertaker of 241 West Twenty-third Street, brought another load from his storage. A rather diverse collection of coffins waited on the pier. Because their own supply of wagons was exhausted, the undertakers had borrowed another twenty wagons from a department store. Men in black, the undertakers assistants provided a very "gloomy army at the end of the pier." The stark white of interns and nurses helped to break up the blackness. New reports of the rescue ship's closing in came every fifteen minutes. At the barely visible outline of the *Carpathia* inching its way into the stream, she was joined by tiny, powerful tugboats that slowly shoved her into her berth. "The docking of *Carpathia* was a perfect piece of seamanship, and her hausers were fastened and her gangplank down with almost unprecedented speed."

"THOUSANDS OF EYES SCAN RAIL" shouted out the *NEWARK NEWS*

"The crowd on the pier pressed forward and thousands of eyes scanned the rail of the ship whose voyage to the other side its commandeer had interrupted to aid in possibly the most humane task a mariner was ever permitted to perform.

Meanwhile, the people waiting for their family or friends, not knowing if they were dead or alive—"had reached a state closely bordering on hysteria." The police were there in force to prevent the mob from overcoming the situation. It was almost 7:30 o'clock—the mob was growing by the minute and poor Inspector McClusky, who was in charge of the police arrangements quickly sent a call to headquarters, where every precinct below Harlam sent policemen in to relieve their weary comrades. The police regulations were perfect. At least 200 automobiles were directed into positions on the pier facing south. The chauffeurs were instructed that when they were leaving with their survivors, they were to move through Thirteenth Street. Then they were further restricted when passes were issued to then proceed past Eleventh Avenue and Fourteenth Street. Then they stopped the trolley west of Fourth Avenue.

It was a scene never witnessed before. The floors of concrete and the steel pillars groaned under the weight of the thousands who had managed to secure passes. The long, long lines waiting at the telephone booths kept breaking into fights from all afternoon on.

Police reserves were being arranged every five feet in lines. Auxiliary cordons intended to fight back those looking for souvenirs were kept busy trying to prevent fakirs and pretenders. Once they showed proof of their right to move on, they were moved to the lettered section, which on ordinary days were reserved for baggage storage and customs inspections. There they stayed waiting for the ship to come in.

It was pouring torrential rain when 7:30 came, and those waiting were informed that the ship would not arrive for another hour and a half. The newspapermen were penned off to one side, growing understandably restless.

CUNARD LINE PIER, NEW YORK

Adding to the information above, a staff correspondent for the *Newark News* continued: "While the *Carpathia* steamed to her dock tonight with ninety-eight dead aboard, an impatient, restless mob stood in the drizzling rain opposite the pier and battled to gain points of vantage. Five hundred mounted and foot policemen with drawn clubs and using scant courtesy in their efforts to preserve a semblance of order with difficulty restrained the multitude, only a small part of which was composed of relatives and friends of the disaster.

"Twenty-five thousand, at least, filled the Cunard Plaza on Eleventh Avenue and intersecting thoroughfares from Twelfth Street to Fifteenth Street, surging like a dense sea as they pushed forward when temporary watchlessness on the part of the officers gave them slight leeway.

"The morbidly curious were, of course, in the vast majority. Those who had real interest in the return of the rescue ship had, for the most part, been taken care of by the Cunard Line and by the customs officials.

As for the 98 dead bodies, we can only assume that they had to follow the law and be embalmed on board ship before docking.

WRECKAGE TELLS TALE OF DISASTER
—*Newark News* April 18, 1912

INDESCRIBABLE PANIC WHEN *TITANIC* STRUCK

SURVIVORS TELL OF MOMENTS OF TERROR

Just prior to *Titanic* hitting the iceberg and FATE stepping in, rendering all on board equal, rich or poor, famous or not, young or old . . . each one had a date with death here—just before that happened, there was a grand gathering in the salon Sunday night. It was for the men and women in First Class only, and attendees dressed to the nines in the latest styles—and clothes in the latest couture, many of which were worn as the passengers stepped into the lifeboats later, or were tossed into the boats, or thrown into the boats, dress clothes and furs. It must have been a sight to see, but not much help or protection from the numbing sheets of water and the violently chilling wind, as the women and children were dropped over the sides of the boat.

The *Carpathia* had by now heard the S.O.S. call, but little did they know they were about to become one of the most famous ships on the sea, as they turned and literally "ran" for *Titanic* location, apparently giving little thought to the imminent danger they themselves were facing, running at top speed through the same field of icebergs that had destroyed *Titanic*. It was full speed ahead, not only for the *Carpathia*, but for each of the other ocean liners that had turned to race to the aid of the sinking ship. They were not in time to see *Titanic* ever again, for she had slipped below the calm surface before they arrived, taking with her the ones whom FATE had chosen for Death.

As the *Carpathia* approached the site of the sinking of **Titanic**, nearly every officer and passenger on board lined the rails looking for signs of life or death in the icy sea. Wreckage floating in that spot was all the *Carpathia* found at that spot. They soon began to see the remains of the shattered ship floating some distance away, while each of the broken pieces seemed to have one or two nearly dead clinging to it. The nearly dead were overcome with the freezing cold, and they perished before they could be saved. The ship chose to go look for survivors rather than dead bodies. They were aided by the feeble cries of the distressed survivors, still clinging to a probable death in the dangerous ice field. The *Carpathia* took in boatloads of survivors and dead bodies. It was reported that "many women were rendered temporarily insane by their harrowing experience and were under care of the physicians in the ocean liner's hospital."

Other stories were told here (New York, April 17—NEWARK NEWS) as calls came in from Wellfleet, Massachusetts as they reported receiving messages from the *Carpathia* that were clear and distinct. She was 250 miles north of Cape Cod at noon. It was thought that she was to be in New York late Thursday night or early Friday.

The *Carpathia* wireless operator made it clear that they had all of the survivors on board found at the scene of the sinking. No other boat had found any survivors in the bitterly freezing icy water. It seems they had about 800 lucky souls on board who had escaped Death.

Stories of unrelenting terror began to follow as a few of the survivors and their rescuers cautiously began to relate small parts of their terrifying experiences. It did not help that the rescue boat was surrounded by oceanic ice, as the survivors could see in their mind's eye some pieces of berg towering "spectre-like" above them, while the crippled ship's "gnashing steel prow" ground into the detached flows of ice which were hitting the sides of the ship, as the "entrapped monster" reversed engines to try to extricate herself.

More stories were shared as they told haltingly of the unwritten law of the seas . . ."Women and Children first." These women and children were snatched from their families, husbands, and fathers, placed in the boats and "lowered over the towering sides of the doomed ship into impenetrable darkness," with only men enough to man the oars of the lifeboats.

Heroic deeds told of in this perilous time include the divine devotion of Mrs. Isador Straus, now among the missing. She chose Death over parting from her husband.

"Rest assured that the names of those rescued will be those of women and children," said P.A.S. Franklin. "There is no rule whereby women and children are rescued first, there is no rule which seafaring men recognize; but it requires no rule to make man stand aside in time of danger. I am confident Captain Smith perished. He is that sort of a man."

SYRIAN WOMAN'S THRILLING NARRATIVE AS TOLD THROUGH AN INTERPRETER

TELLS OF SHIP'S OFFICERS FIRING INTO STEERAGE

Panic amid rush for lifeboats. She says ten people on doomed ship were bound for Ottowa, but only two survive. Story found in encyclopedia-titanica.org.

Mrs. Mariana Assaf, an Ottowa citizen, told a quite interesting and very disturbing story of the Syrians and the treatment they received once the iceberg had destroyed **Titanic**. Mrs. Assaf related a story of terror and catastrophe in her rescue.

"Mariana Assaf arrived in Ottawa from New York at 7:15 last night. She was still ill from the effects of the exposure that had followed her rescue, and the memory of the awful news of the occurrence has left its impact in a disorganized nervous fashion. When she stepped from the Grand Trunk Train which brought her into the capital she gave a cry and sank fainting into the arms of her nephew's wife. Both women were so deeply affected by the reunion that they had to take to their beds and Mrs. Assaf was under a doctor's care when she was seen last night. A woman of 45 years and in appearance a typical Syrian, she bears the marks of that dreadful experience with a haggard air and a voice weak and nervous. At times the wounding memories of the awful events broke out afresh in her mind, her voice becoming hoarse with sobs."

"I was with others of my relations and friends for many of us Syrians on board were known to me and we had all gone to bed when the ship struck. Although it did not seem to be much at first and we did not feel very much at first and we did not feel very much except a jar, some of us

89

wanted to go on deck to see what happened. We were told that everything was all right, and we did not think there was a danger. But the ship did not go on then some of us began to think they were not telling us the truth and that we might be sinking. I think somebody must have said the boat was going to go down for suddenly there was a great confusion and everybody tried to rush the deck. There were many in steerage who tried to rush the boats and at those some of the officers fired revolvers and some of them were shot dead. The rest were driven back. They were not given a chance to escape. As for me, when I thought the ship might sink, I forgot everything and rushed away from steerage and up to the deck where the first class passengers are. I could not think of anything. I never saw any of my relations so I do not know what became of them. The last I saw of them was when we were all in the steerage.

"When I ran up to first class, I saw that the ship must be going to sink and I lost my head. But a man, I think he was one of the sailors, when he saw that I was there, he pushed me into one of the boats where there were already many women and a few men. The boat was lowered into the water and then the men rowed it away for they were afraid that when a big ship went down it would take them with it. Some said the band was playing, but I did not hear it. I was so out of my mind. It was an hour and a half after the boat struck before I was put into a small boat. Then *Titanic* sank and we drifted about all night. It was terribly cold, and I could never forget my relations and my friends whom I would never see again. When I thought of them I felt that I was going to go crazy. Six hours after we left *Titanic* somebody said, 'there's a steamer,' we were saved and we were taken aboard the *Carpathia*. When we got on board the *Carpathia* everyone was very kind and gave me clothes to wear. But I don't remember very much, I could hardly think.

In New York they took me to a Jewish Hospital and I got a little better there. Then the United Syrian Society took me and sent me to Ottawa for I told them that is where I was going. Of those who were coming to Ottawa nearly all were my cousins. When I left Syria to come here again, my two sons wanted to come with me, but I would not let them. Thank GOD I did not, for if they had they would have been drowned . . . they will still be coming out here later with my husband.

One of **Titanic's** lifeboats alongside the *Carpathia*

TITANIC TRAGEDY: Things some people took with them

Major Peuchen left behind $200,000 in bonds, $100,000 in stocks and chose warm clothes instead. Norman Chambers pocketed a revolver and a compass. Steward Johnson took four oranges. Steward Collett placed his Bible in his pocket. The five mail clerks actually dragged over 200 mail sacks up the stairs.

Adolf Dyker handed his wife a satchel with two gold watches, two diamond rings, a sapphire necklace and 200 Swedish crowns. Edith Russell had her musical toy pig. Mrs. Dickson reported, "Steward John Hart struggled to get third class passengers into life jackets and shepherded up the boats. Many still refused to go. As fast as he got them into the boats, they would jump out and go inside where it was warm."

SIX BULLET HOLES *TITANIC* MEMENTOES

**Survivor Tells of being shot at by Officers
while entering Lifeboats**

Wilkes-Barre, PA April 22

The story of having been shot at by officers on *Titanic* while trying to get into a lifeboat when the Great Ship went down was retold today by John Borak (Bert Johns). He was one of only three survivors who came to Wilkes-Barre.

Borak showed a coat with six bullet holes in it that he had worn on the night of the White Star sinking. He managed to get into the last lifeboat. He was picked up by the *Carpathia*.

SIX BULLET HOLES TITANIC MEMENTOES

Newark Star

Tuesday 23 April 1912

Survivor Tells of Being Shot at by Officers While Entering Lifeboat—WILKES BARRE, [sic] Pa., April 22—The story of having been shot at by officers on the Titanic when he sought to enter a lifeboat when the great liner was going down, was told here today by John Borak, one of three survivors who came to this city.

Borak showed a coat with six bullet holes through it, which he had worn on the night when the White Star liner went down. He managed to get into the last lifeboat which put off from the sinking ship and was picked up by the Carpathia.

Mrs. Alexander Thomas, another survivor, told a thrilling story. She became separated from her 6-months-old child in the confusion and refused to get into a boat. Finally an officer told her that another woman had saved the baby. Mrs. Thomas finally found her child among the survivors on the Carpathia.

Related Biographies:
Borak ("Hannah Assi Borah") Hannah
Thamine "Thelma" Thomas
Assad Alexander Thomas/Tannous

Contributor
Mark Baber

TITANIC VICTIMS DIED OF HUNGER

St. Paul Daily News **17 May 1912**

As bizarre as this may seem, a collapsible lifeboat was picked up on May 16 by White Star Liner *Oceanic* which held the bodies of three people. Now this is just a month after the sinking of ***Titanic***.

Clothing worn by one of the victims was later identified as that of Thompson Beattie from Chicago. The other two were crew members.

A grim tale was told by tooth marks on cork and the collapsible lifeboat with dead bodies. Other items were found in the boat: a woman's ring which was inscribed "Edward to Cerda". A fur coat with the name "Williams" in the pocket was found. These items made it clear that there had been others in the boat. The bodies were buried at sea.

All this leads to speculation—how was this lifeboat missed? How was it possible with all the ships that converged on the area, and could there possibly have been others?

.

TITANIC TRAGEDY (biblical-counsel.org)

A deep spiritual significance of the tragedy surfaced in the relating of tales of chivalry and heroism. Steward John Hart struggled to get third class passengers into life jackets and move them on into the boats. According to him, many refused to go. As fast as he got them into the boats, they would jump out and go inside where it was warm.

As the bow of the big ship went down and down, and the stern rising higher out of the water, "a tremendous cacophony erupted of breaking china and glassware, thuds of furniture, the clatter of sliding deck chairs. The lights were out and everything movable in the ship broke.

FOR EVERY WOMAN WHO DIED ON *TITANIC*, THIRTEEN MEN PERISHED.

These are additional first hand short interviews from survivors just stepping off the *Carpathia*. Most are related in their entirety, appropriate credit given. Many of these may have never or seldom been seen in the past 100 years since the sinking. You will note the discrepancy in eyewitness accounts and many contradictions.

GUNFIRE, PANIC REPORTED *TITANIC*

Miss Lily Bentham of Rochester, N. Y., a Second Class passenger, related in the Chicago Daily Journal that the rule "Women and Children" seemed to be happening, allowing the women and children and not the men to get into the lifeboats. When the men tried to get away, she saw shots fired. Miss Bentham was hysterical when the *Carpathia* landed. Mrs. W.J. Douton who also came from Rochester and was a fellow passenger, lost her husband. She tells, "I hadn't been in bed half an hour when the steward rushed down to our cabin and told us to put on our clothes and come up on deck. We were thrown into lifeboats and packed like sardines. As soon as the men passengers tried to get to the boats they were shot at. I don't know who did the shooting. We rowed frantically away from the ship and were tied to four other boats. I arose and saw the ship sinking, the band playing 'Nearer My God To Thee.'

THIRD CLASS MEN SHOT *Chicago Daily Journal* April 19

A New York man, A.A. Dick, said, "Everybody in the first and second cabin behaved splendidly. The members of the crew also behaved magnificently. But some men in the third class, presumably passengers, were shot by some of the officers. Who these men were we do not know. There was a rush for the lifeboats, it was fully an hour after *Titanic* had been struck that the lifeboats were launched. This was due to the fact that those aboard had not the slightest idea that the ship would sink.

HEARD SHOT FIRED *Chicago Daily Journal* April 19

E.W. Beane was a second class passenger. When the lifeboats were lowered, he jumped into the sea. He swam around in the icy water for twenty minutes. "I heard a shot fired, just before I jumped. Afterward I was told a steerage passenger had been shot while trying to leap into a lifeboat filled with women and children."

JUMPED INTO A SMALL BOAT

A steerage passenger named Abraham Hyan who was from Manchester, England, won his safety by leaving steerage and going into the first cabin. "I got alongside of a boat, and as they lowered it, full of passengers, I just crowded in beside the man at the tiller. They could have taken fifteen more people in our boat. There was no commotion in first cabin. I heard a man was shot in a panic in steerage. When our boat got into the water it drifted into the exhaust of the *Titanic* and we were nearly swamped. We rowed off for about half a mile and then saw the lights on the *Titanic* sink gradually out of sight. As the boat sank the lights were down, one after another."

TWO CHINAMEN ARE SHOT TO DEATH
Chicago American April 19

Into one of the last of the lifeboats that were launched, two Chinamen employed in the galley had hidden themselves face down in the bottom of the boat. The women who had been put into the boat were so excitable that they did not notice the presence of the Chinese until the boat had pushed away from the sinking ship.

The Chinamen were found. The officer in charge drew his revolver and shot them both to death and threw them overboard, much to the dismay of the women. The weather was very cold and the sea was filled with floating ice. All were warned before getting into the boats to dress as warmly as possible. Water had by now flooded the engine rooms and the ship was drifting helplessly.

REPORT CAPTAIN A SUICIDE *Chicago Record-Herald* April 19

"Sensational rumors told by hysterical passengers who would not give their names, said that Captain Smith had killed himself on the bridge, that the navel had taken his life and that some Italians were shot in an attempt for the boats. Not confirmed.

ORDERED TO SHOOT MEN *Chicago Record-Herald* April 19

"Everybody to the boats, "was the startling cry that was repeated from end to end of *Titanic*.

"Women and children first" was the hoarse order that sent along the line of lifeboats.

"Shoot the first man who attempts to get into a boat.

Passengers were becoming fear-crazed and flooding the upper decks and gangways amid the horrendous confusion of the first ten minutes. Then the first class passengers rallied to the support of the crew with drawn revolvers. Men who pushed women aside and climbed into the boats were seized and hurled back to the decks or over the rails. Not all first class cabin men were those to struggled to help fight the mob, and some were among those who tried to get into the lifeboats.

REVOLVER SHOTS HEARD *Chicago Record-Herald* April 19

Gunshots from revolvers were heard by many, right before *Titanic* sank. Rumors were that the Captain and First Officer Murdoch had committed suicide. This report was discredited by crew members. Captain Smith was seen last on the bridge just as the ship sank, leaping into the rushing water as the decks washed away.

MAN SHOT SAYS LADY GORDON *Chicago Daily News* April 19

Lady Cosmo Duff Gordon, who left in one of the last of *Titanic's* boats, said that panic had begun to seize some of the remaining passengers by the time her boat was lowered away. "Everyone seemed to be rushing for that boat, nearly the last of all. A few men crowded in and were turned back at the point of Capt. Smith's revolver. Several were felled before order was restored."

"I recall that I was pushed along toward one of the boats and helped in. The boat was lowered past way down on the davits. Just as we were about to clear the ship a man made a rush to get aboard and was shot. He was killed instantly and his body fell into the boat at our feet. No one made an effort to move the body and it remained beneath our feet until we were picked up by the *Carpathia*.

"I saw bodies in the water in all directions. The poor souls could not have lived long, because the water was too cold.

SAD TALES FROM STEERAGE the *Associated Press*

PITIABLE STORIES TOLD BY POORER SURVIVORS IN *TITANIC* DISASTER

New York, April 19. Pitiable tales were related by some of the steerage passengers of *Titanic* as they came off the *Carpathia*. Few of the passengers were met by relatives or friends and a majority were taken in charge by charitable persons. A thrilling story was told by Ellen Shine, a 20-year old girl from County Cork, Ireland, who came here to visit a brother.

"Those who were able to get out of bed," said Miss Shine, "rushed to the upper decks, where they were met by members of the crew, who endeavored to keep them in the steerage quarters. The women, however, rushed by these men, knocking them down, and finally reached the upper decks. When informed that the boat was sinking, most of them fell to their knees and began to pray.

SHOOTS FOUR MEN DEAD *Chicago Inter Ocean* April 19

"I saw one of the lifeboats and made for it. In it were four men from the steerage. They were ordered out by an officer and refused to leave. Then one of the officers jumped into the boat, and drawing a revolver, shot the four men dead. Their bodies were picked from the bottom of the boat and thrown into the sea.

CHICAGO AMERICAN April 20

"We were slung off and the stokers began to row us away. For two hours we cruised around. It did not seem to be very cold. There was no excitement aboard the *Titanic*. We were probably 1000 feet away.

HEARD SEVERAL PISTOL SHOTS

"Suddenly I clutched the sides of the lifeboat. I had seen the *Titanic* give a curious shiver. Almost immediately we heard several pistol shots and a great screaming arise from the decks. Then the boat's stern lifted in the air and there was a tremendous explosion. After this the *Titanic* dropped back again. The awful screaming continued. Two minutes after this there was another great explosion. The whole forward part of the great liner dropped down under the waves. The stern rose a hundred feet, almost perpendicularly. The boat stood up like an enormous black finger against the night sky.

WIDENER WIDOW SAW OFFICER SHOOT SELF

Captain of the *TITANIC* Leaped into the Sea as Great Vessel Sank, Declares Woman Who Lost Her Husband and Son in Sea Tragedy.

SPECIAL DISPATCH TO THE *CHICAGO INTER OCEAN* April 20

Philadelphia, PA April 19

In describing her experience in the sinking of *Titanic*, Mrs. George D. Widener, whose husband, a wealthy financier of this city, and their son were drowned, said that she had seen Captain Smith of the liner jump from the bridge into the sea, and that, a moment before, she had seen another officer turn a revolver upon himself and send a bullet into his brain.

"Mr. Widener and I had retired to our cabin for the night when the shock of crashing into the iceberg occurred. We thought little of it and did not leave our cabin. We must have remained there an hour before coming fearful. Then Mr. Widener went to our son Harry's room and brought him to our cabin.

GAVE AID TO OFFICERS

"A short time later Harry went on deck and hurried back and told us that we must go on deck. Mr. Widener and Harry a few minutes later went on deck and aided the officers, who were then having trouble with those in steerage. That was the last I saw of my husband or son.

"I went on deck and was put into a lifeboat. As the boat pulled away from the *Titanic*, I saw one of the officers shoot himself in the head, and a few minutes later saw Captain Smith jump from the bridge into the sea.

BOTH LOST THEIR LIVES

Mr. Widener and his son Harry were among the victims of the disaster. Mrs. Widener is at her home at Elkins Park, PA, near here. The entire Widener family, which is among the most prominent in Philadelphia's financial and social circles, is overcome by the disaster. The family has received messages of sympathy from all parts of the world.

DODGE SAW TWO MEN SHOT *CHICAGO INTER OCEAN* April 20

San Francisco Millionaire, Saved With Family, Tells of Outbreak

Washington Dodge, millionaire financier of San Francisco, with his wife and 6-year-old son, were among those saved from the wrecked ship.

"There was no panic of any description except in the steerage. I saw two frenzied men shot down by officers as they tried to fight their way into a lifeboat. That was the only outbreak I saw."

Washington Dodge was one of the most picturesque personages saved from *Titanic*.

HEADLINES FROM *NEWARK NEWS* April 1912

Carpathia Captain reluctantly spoke with our reporter who questioned him as to why the news of the wreck and the condition of the survivors had been withheld. "You have not given out the news and we have waited a week. Will you let me get it now?"

"You stay on this bridge with me or I will put you in irons . . . I won't talk to you . . . you came on board this boat in spite of orders from a thousand sources, and I won't be criticized by you," said the Captain of the *Carpathia*.

HUGE CROWD JAMS STREETS IN A BATTLE TO GREET SURVIVORS

Amid Scenes Such as Never Before Were Equaled, Rescued Passengers from the *TITANIC* describe Horrors of Catastrophe and Suffering by Woman and Children.

CROWD SEIZED BY FRENZY

FIRST ACT OF MANY WHEN THEY FIRST SET FOOT ON LAND IS TO MUTTER THANKS TO ALMIGHTY, THEN STORY OF DISASTER IS GASPED OUT IN SENTENCES THAT ADD TO WORLD GRIEF.

TITANIC DEATH TOTAL NOW FIXED AT 1,400. LINER RACING TO PORT WITH SURVIVORS.

PROPERTY LOSS SO COLOSSAL FIGURES SCARCELY CAN CONVEY IT TO HUMAN MIND.

IF ONLY

"If only" *Titanic* had paid more attention to the iceberg warnings . . . if only the last warning had even reached the bridge . . . if only the wireless operator hadn't cut off one final attempt to reach her . . . if only the men in the crows' nest had binoculars . . . if only they had sighted ice seconds earlier or seconds later . . . if only there had been enough lifeboats . . . if only the watertight bulkheads had gone one deck higher . . . if only the ship on the horizon had come closer that night . . . if only they had not switched to another route . . . if only the ship had practiced a drill . . . if only the passengers knew exactly what to do in an emergency . . . if only . . . if only . . . IF ONLY.

"It is not given to everyone to be a hero." (Nautical Magazine)

D-Day—Date with Death—April 14, 15

The ice hit; the boat went down with a great loss of life. No one could believe the Queen of the Sea was going to sink.

The water was 31 degrees—the air was 32 degrees.

Judge Not

And so we reach the end of this story. The deep blue sea holds *Titanic* now, and she will not easily give up her secrets. She lies alone today, at the bottom of the sea, exactly as she has for the last 100 years . . . virtually untouched by the hands of TIME . . . fish and other sea creatures have eaten away at anything edible. Shipwreck explorers have even gone aboard with modern robotics, trying to determine exactly what happened on that fateful night in April 1912.

Anyone who was on the Great Ship that night is now dead. No one exists today who can tell us firsthand the truth of that night. She is *Titanic*. She has no match anywhere. She only took the one ride, but what a ride it was.

The bow of the wrecked *RMS Titanic*, photographed in June 2004
(Wikipedia)

**The story of Bert Johns sets one record straight
after 100 long years.**

Some called him a coward, along with every other man who survived the sinking of the Mighty *Titanic*. As long as the story of *Titanic* was fresh, these men were constantly scorned and harassed.

Bert Johns was a fine young man. He couldn't speak any English at all. He took a chance when he saw empty seats in a lifeboat that was leaving. Live or Die? He chose to give living another chance. He was shot six times—his coat was his witness—six bullet holes. His friends were who knows where, everyone was pushing, shouting, shoving, screaming, kicking . . . the scene was totally unreal.

I say, "Judge Not, lest YOU be judged." Unless you were there . . . unless you walked in each man's shoes . . . unless you were one of the chosen to be on the maiden voyage of the Mighty *Titanic*, undisputed

Queen of the Seas, you have no right to criticize, or call names, or throw stones. All of the boat riders are now dead. After 100 years, it is now to us the living to finally forgive and forget. It is impossible for us to walk in their shoes—none of us really know what they would do if they had been there—the yelling, the screaming, the pushing, the shoving, the crying, the gunshots, the raging sea rushing in, and the gates some say were locked.

The time has finally come for everyone to let it go, and to realize that each and every one on the Ship of Dreams, the Ship of Fools, was no Coward.

The Dream and then the Nightmare, The Syrians who boarded the Titanic

"For the fortunate ones (Syrians) who survived the sinking of *Titanic*, the story has been told for almost 100 years, and it is said today in Lebanon and Syria, that even though their countrymen were lucky to survive and did not perish in the icy waters of the Atlantic, they were swallowed up by the new world. Many left never to return, while those who did return, came as visitors to see family and friends. A few, like *Mubarik Hanna Sulayman Abi Asi* (Bert Johns) returned to their homeland to live out their final years in the land of their birth."

(The above does not agree with Bert Johns obituary. It appears not to be true, for he stayed in Michigan until his death and burial in Port Huron, Michigan, in 1952.)

However, the book entitled The Dream and then the Nightmare, The Syrians who boarded the *Titanic* was reviewed by George Jacub in *The Titanic Review* (encyclopedia titanica). He reveals that the story is filled "with information never before available . . . it sprinkles the story with controversy—firsthand evidence of the darkest secret of the *Titanic* disaster" . . . the deliberate mistreatment of Syrians.

This book makes it clear that very little is known about the Syrians on board. According to Jacub, "They were poor, they didn't speak English, and they had funny (to us) names." They retold stories of Syrians being shot and not being let into the lifeboats . . . even being singled out for abuse.

Much of that appears to be likely to have happened.

Yusuf Naum al-Khuri said that Bert Johns told him, "Fellow countrymen from Hardin were courageous until the end and remained calm in the face of DEATH."

This story is told today in Hardin, Lebanon: "Few noticed the woman dressed in elegant clothing who approached Bert Johns and called to him to enter a lifeboat with her." "When the last two lifeboats were lowered, Bert Johns leapt through the guards and plunged over the side of the ship. Women took pity on the young man and covered him with their skirts."

According to Dhawg Dagher, who was proud to tell this story of his sister Aminah . . . she helped a foreign lady hide Bert Johns. They all held their breath hoping he would not be seen. Aminah hid him under her loose and wide clothing.

.

Additional information on Bert Johns

Bert Johns' first address in Port Huron was with Mr. Hassey @ 1119 11th Avenue.

Bert's *Titanic* ticket: No.2663 . . . It probably cost somewhere between 7 and 9 pounds.

CERTIFICATE OF DEATH

MICHIGAN DEPARTMENT OF HEALTH
Vital Records Section

7702 13417

JOHN

BERT
1885 — 1952

ELIZABETH
1892 — 1970

Bert John
Survivor Of
The Titanic
1912

THANKS:

I would like to thank Bert John's Port Huron area family for their contribution to this story . . . Dianne Johns and her mother Theresa Johns of Fort Gratiot . . . Josephine Mericka and Gloria Olson of Port Huron.

His experience was so traumatic, Josephine confided, while Theresa Johns related that it was a nightmare . . . Gloria remembers sitting with him in his bar, and while Dianne never met him, his story has always remained with her.

Theresa and Dianne were gracious and friendly, allowing us the use of family pictures for Bert's book.

REFERENCES

BOOKS:

The Night Lives On Walter Lord

A Night to Remember Walter Lord

The Dream and then the Nightmare, The Syrians who boarded the Titanic Leila Salloum Elias

Report on the Loss of the S.S. TITANIC Official British Government Enquiry

Wreck and Sinking of the Titanic: The Ocean's Greatest Disaster Marshall Everett

The truth about the Titanic Archibald Gracie

Raise the Titanic! Clive Cussler

ADDITIONAL WEBSITES:

findagrave.com titanichistoricalsociety.com

Wikipedia: Timeline of the Sinking of the TITANIC

TITANICresearch.com

Encyclopediatitanica.com

The TITANIC Lifeboats Project—John M Hennessey titanic/lifeboats

Snopes.com

Historyonthenet.com/TITANIC

Groups.yahoo.com/group TITANIC

NEWSPAPERS:

Chicago Tribune

Newark News/ Newark Star

New York Times TITANIC book

MOVIES:

SAVED FROM THE TITANIC (1912)

TITANIC (1953)

A NIGHT TO REMEMBER (1958)

TITANIC (1999)

NATIONAL GEOGRAPHIC . . . SECRETS OF THE TITANIC:
ANNIVERSARY EDITION (1912)

About the Author

The author was born in Detroit, Michigan, in October of 1949, the third of four children of Harold and Marjorie Johnson. Harold was from Albion, New York, where his great-grandfather had come in on the opening of the Erie Canal and settled at a place called The Bridges, New York. Harold came to Michigan to work in the automobile plants during the Depression, where he met and married Marjorie Dawson, who was in the city attending Beauty School. In 1957 they returned to her hometown in Marlette in the Thumb of Michigan and bought the family farm started by Grandfather William Dawson in 1882.

Lois graduated from Marlette High School in 1967, Salutatorian and Class Treasurer. She pursued her college education at Oakland University in Rochester, Michigan, receiving a Bachelor of Arts in Elementary Education in 1971. Although she was offered the newly formed position of Director of Alumni at OU, it was only a half-time position then, and she instead went to work for Warren Consolidated Schools as a Math/Science teacher at Grissom Junior High on 14 Mile and Ryan, beginning her first real job walking the picket line, on strike. Pink-slipped at the end of her first year teaching, Lois returned to the Thumb and spend the next 27 years teaching Math, then Social Studies and Reading, to 6th graders, taking Early Retirement in 1998. She earned a Master's Degree from Central Michigan University, and 18 hours towards her Specialist's.

In the early 1970's she purchased 50 acres of the family Centennial Farm, turning it into a Michigan Non-Profit Wildlife Sanctuary, where she now raises beautiful free-ranging peacocks on one of the most lovely spots on earth.

In 1985, Lois happened to visit a stunning old Victorian House in town, where she was amazed to learn that it had been built by her mother's Great-Uncle, Thomas Usher Dawson, Marlette's leading businessman in the 1890's. That started her on a quest for family information that ultimately led to the town's newspaper office, *The Marlette Leader,* where she found the old copies of the newspapers. It was that visit that eventually sparked enough interest that she convinced the newspaper editor, John Frazier, to help her start *The Marlette Historical Society and Museum.* They then microfilmed the old newspapers, and had three Marlette buildings named to the State Historic Sites Registry: the Victorian House of Thomas Usher and Jennie Dawson; the Marlette First United Methodist Church, and the 1890 Marlette Depot. They wrote grants for a museum, bought the old depot and did everything necessary for its restoration, thanks to two additional grants from the State of Michigan and M-DOT. 1987 was the 150th of the State of Michigan, the 125th of the City of Marlette, and the 100th Year of the High School, which they commemorated with a 432-page book, in conjunction with the High School Yearbook, IMAGES. Lois then followed up on that book with an 820-page Millennium Edition.

She adopted 12-year old twins in 1989. She was named to Who's Who Among America's Teachers in 2000 and again in 2005, an honor given to less than 3% of America's Elementary Teachers.

She wrote of her father's friendship with the World's Greatest Santa Claus, Charlie Howard, in the book, My Dad Knew Santa Claus. Charles Howard, of Albion, New York, who unbelievably held 5 million children on his lap, was the famous Macy's Santa who started the World's Only School for Santas and the wonderland for children, Christmas Park, the unequaled Santa Claus Headquarters of the World. Howard died in 1966, when he was entered into the United States Congressional Record as the Dean of Santa Claus. It is an adult story for the child in each of us.

The women of my town, Marlette, Michigan, made a huge US flag of 34 stars which they sent off to the Civil War with a man named Thomas Henry Sheppard. He guarded that flag with his life all through the war, as it became the Battle Flag of the First Michigan Cavalry. They survived 13 major battles, over 100 skirmishes, sixteen months of war, then 505 days as a POW, after he was taken captive after the Greatest Battle of the Civil War, riding right behind General Custer as the

First Michigan Cavalry stopped the surprise attack of Col. Hampton's men, and effectively prevented Pickett's Charge from succeeding.

To top that, in 1884, the War's Greatest Volunteer General, John Logan, was running for the Vice-Presidency of the United States. He crossed the country on his Whistle-Stop campaign, stopping at every little train station, giving his 5-minute campaign speech, and ending with his favorite story of a nameless volunteer who went off to war carrying a flag made by the women of his town. When he came to my town, the coincidental meeting between these two men was extraordinary.

<u>He Kept the Colors/The True Story of the General, the Old Man and the Flag</u>

Lightning Source UK Ltd.
Milton Keynes UK
UKHW012127270720
367273UK00002B/9/J